£1

NAKED APE 2

an anthology
of sexism
collected by the
Guardian

edited by
Aidan White

with an introduction by
Victoria Wood

D1337535

DUCKWORTH

First published in September 1982
Second Impression September 1982
Gerald Duckworth & Co. Ltd.,
The Old Piano Factory,
43 Gloucester Crescent, London NW1

Designed by Sasha Devas

ISBN 0 7156 1685 4

Printed in Great Britain by
Redwood Burn Ltd., Trowbridge, Wiltshire, and
bound by Pegasus Bookbinding, Melksham, Wiltshire

Contents

How much more will Trudi & Jo be revealing this year?

MUCH MORE
THAN YOU'D IMAGINE!
STAND 2311
INTERBUILD

ORIGINAL
SHOWERLUX

Advert for Showerlux, Builders Merchants Journal

Introduction

Dear Readers,

You don't know me. I'm Victoria Wood's neighbour, and I just nipped in to see if she had any Prune Sorbet (the varnish not the pudding, need I add) and I caught sight of these clippings at the back of the filing cabinet, and I thought you might be interested to hear what I thought about it all. I mean, presumably the book is aimed at me, a woman of today (and anyway, let's face it, it's we girls that do the shopping). If Victoria were here, no doubt she'd proffer her comments too, but presumably she's upstairs writing one of her wry ditties about relationships. (My husband's not struck with her style of humour, but he doesn't mind me watching).

Now, without wishing to land right in with a criticism, I do feel I should tell you this kind of book is really rather out of date. I mean, Women's Lib was absolutely yonks ago, wasn't it? Before midi-skirts. Of course, there was a lot about it you couldn't take seriously, and really if you go without a bra long enough, you've only yourself to blame if your husband leaves you for a perkier pair. But it made me think twice and I did change from underwired to seamless, thus giving a smoother line under T-shirts and tops of a similar knitted fabric. The burning I didn't hold with, feeling they would have been better bundled up and air-lifted to underdeveloped countries. (My husband said if they were underdeveloped they didn't need bras anyway, which shows a lot of give and take, I think). To be fair, Germaine Greer did show a lighter side in that television show with Kenny Everett. (And I don't know who he's married to, but he looks like he wouldn't know a square meal if it hit him on the shoulder).

But getting back to the book, it looks awfully well put together and so on, but times have changed bookwise. Obviously, I'm not a publisher, but I would have thought something short about someone getting their sight back, or fibre, would have been a safer bet for Christmas. And really, it wasn't as if women were the underdogs any more. There'll always be snide remarks from both parties (you should hear my sister on the subject of nose-hair) but things are marvellous as compared with earlier. When I was first married, I spent all day scrubbing my husband's collars, lugging heavy shopping bags and worrying over suet. Now I have a hatchback and a freezer, I can shop in bulk and if I were to drop dead tomorrow, Ken would have enough frozen dinners for him not to have to call on his mother for three weeks.

To put it in its historical perspective, I often think how pleased Mrs Pankhurst would be to see me with my spray-on stain remover, enabling me to loosen everyday grime without soaking.

One important point re liberation. Behind every liberated woman is a tolerant husband. (Single women I won't go into, because obviously they throw themselves into their work due to having no one to please). I'm lucky. My husband is a real man of today. He knows where I keep the hoover, and brings it out for me every Sunday morning, often without being asked (though obviously I have to go back for the attachments myself). He will always use an ashtray, and if I have forgotten of my own accord to place one on the arm of his chair, he is quite happy to call out and ask me to bring one (I must admit this has only happened since turn-ups went out of fashion).

He does a marvellous fried egg, and when I was in bed for a day with pneumonia he very kindly left one outside the door for me. And yes he did stack the pans by the sink ready for me to wash the next day. If there's something on the TV I like and he's not keen on (documentaries or plays regarding birth) I'm quite at liberty to watch it on the black and white in the spare room and no hard feelings. It is warm enough in there if you sit in the sleeping bag.

Obviously, equality is fine when Britain's on its feet, but in terms of unemployment and recession we must think again. If a man and a woman are up for the same job, she should step aside (because, let's face it, leave a man at home on his own and he'll mope, whereas a woman in the same situation can at least keep herself happy re-lining the kitchen shelves).

And don't let feminism go too far. I for one would be very sad if a building site worker no longer felt he had the automatic right to comment on my bust line.

Be reasonable, girls. Do you really want to find yourself understanding politics and walking on the outside of the pavement?
Think on.

Mrs K. Smith
(V. Wood's husband's neighbour)

Burger bar advert

6

Editor's Foreword

Each week up to 300 letters turn up on the Naked Ape desk at the *Guardian*. A vast army of Ape hunters keeps our weekly column well stocked with prime examples of the Apish art, perfected by men and performed in a world of Me-Tarzan-You-Jane.

But Naked Ape is not just a catalogue of clangers, a comic diversion. It is a reminder that – out there – the attitudes of the dark age, of sexual inequality still prevail. In spite of equal pay and sex discrimination laws women are still worse off than the other half. Men receive, on average, 30 per cent more in their pay packets and they have all the best jobs.

Who can be surprised to find Naked Ape at work in Parliament, in the courts or in business when only 3 per cent of MPs, 3.9 per cent of High Court judges, and 2.3 per cent of company directors are women? It is the same story at school: while 59 per cent of all teachers are women, only 16 per cent of them are head teachers in secondary schools.

The list is endless: only 14 per cent of dentists and 4 per cent of architects are women, and women make up a minute part of the engineering workforce – 0.5 per cent. On the other hand . . . three out of four boring office jobs in the country are held by women.

Though women might make up 40 per cent of the total workforce, the attitudes reflected in this second volume of *Naked Ape* show that on the whole men preserve for them idiot status. No one, no matter how hi-falutin the title – judge, police chief, archbishop, regius professor, general secretary or Privy Councillor – is untouched by the scraggy, old-fashioned idea that women are not up to much bar child-bearing (sons, please) and . . . sex.

But things are beginning to change. We gratefully acknowledge the contributions from readers that have made this little teaching aid possible. We intend to spend some of the money made from the sale of the book on a modest project which might assist in winkling Ape out of the media.

The Guardian, Farringdon Road, London, E.C.1.   Aidan White

Pretty... boring

Containers advertisement

In Judgment

FOR INDECENT assault on a girl aged between 13 and 16 the maximum penalty is two years' imprisonment. For indecent assault on a boy under 16 the maximum penalty is 10 years imprisonment.

Parliamentary answer to question on paedophilia

WIVES might be infuriating at times — but that was no excuse to stick forks in their necks, said Sheffield magistrate Gilbert Willis.

Sheffield Star

AN OSTEOPATH was jailed five years yesterday for raping his former lover during what was described as an 'horrific seven-hour ordeal of sex and violence'. The victim had lived with the accused for two years, a fact which judge Christopher Beaumont said he had taken in account in reducing the sentence substantially'.

Daily Telegraph

Compensation: Psychological Impotence – The appellant was aged 42 in 1977 when he was injured by being kicked twice in the testicles. The particulars of personal injury were bruising, pain and suffering. However, he suffered from psychological impotence. At the time of the hearing he was aged 46, married with a family ranging from 19 to 7 years. He gave evidence that he could no longer achieve an erection and this was causing considerable marital stress. Award: £22,500 reduced to £17,500 on the basis that had he sought treatment it might have had some success.

Compensation: Nervous Shock – The appellant was a nurse aged 17 in 1979 when she was assaulted and raped three times. At the time she was 10 weeks pregnant. As a result of the attack she was bruised and suffered severe shock and upset. She could no longer accept her pregnancy and an abortion was carried out. She now has difficulty assessing the motives of men. Her social life has become more limited. Award: £5,000.

Bulletin of Northern Ireland Law 1981

Pc was punched

Lorry driver Harry Gregory dragged his wife from a taxi and punched a policeman who came to her rescue.

Passers-by helped Pc Howard Ash in the struggle to free the unconscious women, magistrates at Buxton heard.

Gregory, aged 50, of Crabtree Avenue, Waterfoot Rossendale, was fined £70 for assaulting the officer and £30 for assaulting Mrs Andrea Gregory. He was ordered to pay £54.95 for her damaged clothes.

Manchester Evening News

In his judgment Mr. Justice French said there was no doubt that the injury caused was a dreadful one which would have longlasting consequences for Dawn.Here employment prospects would be severely limited.

However, he found her a bright, cheerful, and charming little girl and said that he had no doubt that if she wished to marry and have children she would be able to cope.

Western Times and Gazette

The judge had told the jury of eight women and seven men: "If a woman voluntarily consumes alcohol to such an extent as to be virtually insensible, it is not rape to have intercourse with such a woman, just as it is not rape to have intercourse with a sleeping woman.

When a woman was drunk but not insensible, the matter was different. "In such situations what you must determine is whether intercourse took place forcibly and against her will."

The Guardian

A SENIOR Old Bailey judge for the first time in his career gave a man probation for rape . . . Twenty-year-old Trevor Johnson had rescued a young girl from a beating by her boyfriend only to rape her himself. Judge Buzzard told Johnson he was satisfied that it was an 'exceptional case of rape' and that he had started off with the best of intentions towards the girl.

Enfield Independent

A HUSBAND who kicked in a plate glass shop window claimed it was an accident because he had intended to kick his wife instead, but missed.

Atherstone Herald

In Court

INSTEAD OF hitting his wife during an argument, a youth took his temper out on a neighbour's car. Edward James Michelle, 17, of Grove Street Wantage, pleaded guilty to criminal damage.

Oxford Mail

Mr David Nathan, defending, said the man might have been forgiven for thinking he would end up in bed with the secretary.

"The days of Sir Walter Raleigh are gone, and men don't carry strange ladies' washing and have coffee with them unless they think they are on to a good thing," he added.

News of the World

A GIRL needed her lip stitched after she was struck twice across the face in a "cowardly and mean" attack by her boyfriend. "The case at first sight appears to be a lover's tiff," said Mr Gray, prosecuting "but the prosecution cannot fail to say how shocked we were that this boy should strike his girlfriend who is only 15. Women can be difficult and tiresome at times, but no young man should act in the way that he did."

Tamworth Herald

Mr Elikkos Georghiades, defending, claimed bottom-touching was no longer indecent: "Many young ladies have had their bottoms touched in jest. And I daresay that some of the gentlemen of the jury have touched ladies bottoms in jest as well.

"But indecent assault is a very strong word.

Islington Gazette

Fined £2 for indecent exposure

At **Carrickmacross District Court** yesterday, Eric Smyth (31), an unemployed married man of 4 Cloughvalley, Carrickmacross, Co Monaghan, who pleaded guilty to indecent exposure and to making rude suggestions to three schoolgirls, was fined £2 by District Justice T. P. O'Reilly.

Earlier the court fined him £10 for siphoning a gallon of petrol from a car at McQuillan's garage on September 21st last.

Irish Times

Mr Lewis Jones (prosecuting) said Mrs O'Kane, had come home one night to find her husband drunk. There was an argument and he punched her in the face knocking her to the ground.

He then tried to force her head down a lavatory and after failing to do this he kicked her on the head causing bruising and swelling.

Mr Jones added that a 12-month prison sentence had been suspended for two years less than 12 months ago when Mr O'Kane had stabbed his wife in the leg with a carving knife.

He said on that occasion she had needed nine stitches to two wounds.

Mr Richard Duckham (defending) said the two offences had been purely matrimonial difficulties.

Warrington Guardian

11

Out of Court

POLICE had to be called in after a row erupted between protesters and Tendring councillors on Monday night over their policy towards battered women.

There was uproar after a remark by housing services committee chairman Mr Richard Fairley in reply to repeated interruptions from the packed public gallery.

Rising to his feet, an annoyed Mr Fairley (Con, Lawford and Manningtree) told one woman campaigner — herself a victim of a beating — that he felt sorry for her husband.

And in defence of his views about the treatment of battered women, he explained: "I am a countryman and nature has its own way of dealing with it."

East Sussex Gazette

IS A man morally blameless for killing women and children if he honestly believes such acts are necessary in the cause of liberation?

Discussion Question from Ethics and Belief by Peter Baelz

IT HAS been pointed out that, where corporal punishment is used, exceptions are in any event made in respect of girls and children suffering from a disability.

Sir Vincent Evans in his dissenting opinion in the Court of Human Rights report on corporal punishment

Two police officers arrived, but he refused to come quietly. The policeman backed off, but the policewoman cornered him by climbing a wall, which was much appreciated by those of us watching."

The Advertiser, Southampton

POLICE WERE playing it cool for today's race march in Swindon. Several churches support the aims of the march and the Bishop of Malmesbury, Freddy Temple, is sending his wife along.

Swindon Evening Advertiser

Inside

Wife-bashing
— sport
or sickness
See Page 22

Orpington Times

HOW MUCH more sensible it would have been if the Chief Constable concerned had defended the language used by his detectives as being wholly in accordance with majority usage, however much it may shock unrepresentative female libbers whose own way of talking and thinking offends popular susceptibilities far more deeply than any loud-mouthed policeman.

Peregrine Worsthorne, The Row Over Rape, Sunday Telegraph.

Barrister and woman found dead

Blyth Morning Telegraph

"A lot of these girls really ask for it", said a spokesman for Scotland Yard, which is actively campaigning to bring home to youngsters the possible perils of hitch-hiking.

"They are pretty. They dress provocatively, get into a car with a bored, lonely man — and then wonder why he starts making advances."

Halifax Courier

In Marriage

Choosing her Bridal Gown is one of the most important decisions a girl will ever make.

Hounslow Informer

PRINCE CHARLES has waived the right of Princess Di to her own pay packet from the taxpayer. *The Sun*

Twenty years ago most self respecting brides would accept a brief smacking about the head and shoulders on spilling the old man's brown ale. Not so today. Women know their rights, God help us.

Bedfordshire on Sunday

'300,000 women are living in sin'

By A. J. McILROY

A GOVERNMENT survey has shown that at least a third of a million women under the age of 50 are living with men outside marriage.

The sample survey disclosed that most women find it difficult to tell the interviewers that they are cohabiting. They passed themselves oc at first as being married to the man with whom they were living.

Daily Telegraph

If a wife wants to keep a husband alive to her attractions she should treat herself like the living room wall — and every now and then THAT needs to be stripped and redecorated !

Lucy Ashton, Sunday Express

But **Mr Anthony Bush,** spokesman for the Bristol Family Life Association said there was certainly truth in the report.

"I think a lot of married men are unfaithful to their wives," he said.

Blame

"I don't blame them entirely. It takes two to make an infidelity.

"Wives don't realise the sexual urges of their men, and don't try hard enough to meet them.

"Women need love where men need sex and sometimes women are able to find love without sex."

Bristol Evening Post

Fornicate: commit fornication, - a'tion n. sexual intercourse between a man and an unmarried woman.

Readers Digest Pocket Dictionary

ALMOST A quarter of all divorces in Britain involve couples who have been married for more than 20 years . . . when presumably one of the partners (more likely to be the wife) has lost a great deal of their sex appeal.

Letter, Sunday Times of Malta

Oxford Area Yellow Pages

It's not surprising that ardent women's libbers should demand that a girl baby should be next in line to the Throne after the Prince of Wales. You would expect them to believe that a future brother should not displace her.

What is surprising is that normally more serious people should agree.

Woodrow Wyatt, Sunday Mirror

AND I confess I am sorry for the husband whose wife has "money of her own", and who is not allowed to forget it. A wife who dominates or humiliates her husband because she happens to "have the money" ought to be kicked.

Guide to Marriage, by Leslie J. Tizard

THE BRIDE'S mother must be very proud to have got rid of three daughters in as many years.

BBC Royal Wedding commentary

Safety Film ad, Harlow Star

Lost career

When I first met my husband at art college we both had equally promising career prospects. I gave it all up when I married, and we now have two teenage children. He is very successful, and we have an interesting social life, but I am always introduced just as 'his wife'. I feel frustrated. I know I could have done so well if I had had the same chance.
Mrs S D, Nottingham.

I have little time for women who moan about their successful husbands. He might not have taken advantage of those lucky breaks, you know. Then where would you be? The happiest wives I know are those who enjoy being complementary to their men. Can't you smile and take pleasure and pride in reflected glory? He must need a perfect hostess, so enjoy being one. Feeling martyred will make you bitter.

Dear Katie (Boyle) TV Times

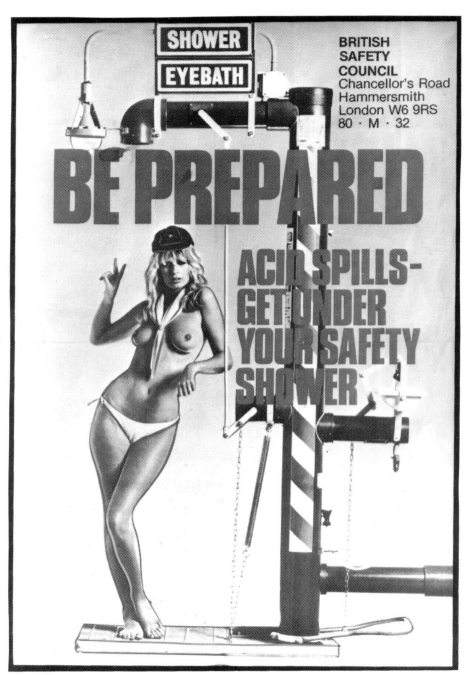

British Safety Council

Ape about the House

SEWING BEANS is a back-breaking sort of job and so I suggest you find some children to do this. Failing that, get the wife on it.

Go Gardening with Harold Lewis, Gloucestershire Echo

BIRTH CONTROL has helped to fuel women's lib which has ravaged the family unit. All our members are very opposed to role-swapping: fathers changing nappies and that sort of thing.

Dr Adrian Rodgers of Responsibility in Welfare, Wolverhampton Express and Star

CL: Do you do housework?
AS: No.
CL: Why not?
AS: Because I don't want to, I'm too busy and it is understood between my wife and I that that's her job not mine.
CL: When you're at home, what do you do?
AS: Mostly watch television.

Arthur Scargill, interviewed in City Limits

WE'VE a friend who quite often comes to polish his shoes at our house. Somehow, the one thing his wife never remembers to buy is shoe polish.

Letter, Sunday Post

A Barnsley man explained the hostile reaction. The shop, he said, was opposite a school and near an old people's home. "The Barnsley miner is a puritan at heart," he said. "He may go out,

drink 15 pints and go home and beat his wife, but he is still a puritan."

The Guardian

PRACTICAL LIVING: written mainly for women or DIY beginners – but just as useful for experts or men.

Art Guild Magazine

Women will love it!

It is written by a man (brave fellow), and his attitudes to housework are revolutionary. Using his methods (and he knows - he employs 2,000 cleaners) women can save up to 75% of the time they spend on cleaning. We've tried his methods ourselves - and believe us - they work.

Advert for Is there Life After Housework, The Bookseller

IT IS through these channels that French regional cooking has evolved, the recipes handed down from one family to another, from mother to daughter, and in the case of professional restaurateurs, from father to son.

Bon Appetit, BBC Publications

> 'We never used to argue but now we regularly fall out,' said Stan, from his council home in Tiverton.
> 'She gets mad because I sit around the house with nothing to do. At least she's got the housework.'

Sunday Independent

THIS *birianee*, though somewhat complicated, is meant for the big occasion when you want to do someone really well, like the boss who, you hope, will give your husband a rise . . .

The Complete Book of Curries, Harvey Day

CATERING IS wide open. Just as every little woman who has had it off with her husband considers at some point taking up sex as a profession.

Clement Freud MP, in Punch

NEVER SKIMP the amount of beating. Ices, like women, dogs and walnut trees, are always improved by consistent walloping.

Fanny and Johnny Craddock's Freezer Book

COUNCIL CHIEF Gordon Moore has warned his wife and family that he will leave them to survive as best they can if Britain comes under nuclear attack.

As chief executive of Bradford he has a place reserved in a control shelter. "There is no way they could enter the shelter with me," Mr Moore said. "It would be chaotic to have women and children running around a control room."

News of the World

> A mere glance at a Neff is sufficient to make some women reach for their husbands' wallets.

Oven Advertisement, The Times

THE COMPLETE KITCHEN

In this day and age a kitchen is no longer just a place to do the cooking and household chores, but where a woman can call it her domain, be proud of and enjoy working in.

Advert for New Forest Kitchens

If you want a new bathroom smother him with kisses.

Advertisement for bathroom equipment

Advertising circular

Politics

IF YOU are away from home on May 6 (election day) do apply for your postal vote, and also for your wife's if she is accompanying you.

Newcastle North Conservative Association Letter

AS A mark of his own decisiveness he has become a fully paid up member of the SDP. "I also made my wife Daphne a member," he says.

John Rae, Headmaster of Westminster school, Sunday Telegraph

WOMEN HAVE never had it so good the Commons was told by Mrs Shiela Faith the MP for Belper . . . the greatest assistance to women was the 1956 Clean Air Act, said Mrs Faith. It meant there was less dust and women now spent less time cleaning up.

Derby Evening Telegraph

THE COUNCIL approved a Labour motion from Mrs Jackie Lawton directing that the wearing of school uniform should no longer be compulsory. Miss Lawton wore a fetching red dress – ideologically sound – which set off her dark hair and eyes.

Leicester Mercury

PEOPLE, WOMEN in particular I believe, have a reputation in the broadcasting world for never changing the station on their radios because they fear that they will never find it again.

Baroness Trumpington, in House of Lords debate

FASHION WAS the talking point for many observers when Premier met President in London yesterday. Margaret Thatcher wore a tailored suit, printed blouse and pearls. President Vigdis Finnbogadottir of Iceland was smart too. She was wrapped in fur for the start of a five-day visit.

Daily Mirror

LET US put aside the Chancellor's style. He can't help it. He was born with it. He will never be the sort of orator who makes men jump on their wives with excitement.

Terence Lancaster, Daily Mirror

WHAT CAUSES most distress to the residents is the kerb-crawlers, molesting their womenfolk.

James Hill MP, Radio 4

Mr Stokes: In view of the large number of unemployed fathers supporting wives and young children, should not some women in well-paid jobs who are married to men examine their consciences and decide whether in the circumstances they might give up their jobs?

Mr Alison: I am glad that my Hon. Friend added the rider that they are married to men. No doubt if the wife was married to my Hon. Friend she would undoubtedly be persuaded to give up work. For the rest it is by no means certain that the kind of jobs – largely part-time – in service industries that women might vacate would be suitable for or sought after by men.

Oral question to Minister of State Mr Michael Alison, Hansard

Foot picks his men

By Julia Langdon,
Political Correspondent

Mr Michael Foot moved yesterday to explode the charge that his opposition spokesmen do not reflect Labour Party policy. He announced the appointment of a unilateralist, Mr John Silkin, to the Shadow defence post, and gave Mr Eric Heffer—a committed European though anti-marketeer—responsibility for European and Community Affairs.

These two appointments in Mr Foot's new team of principal Shadow spokesmen were clearly intended to confront the criticism on the left of the party—

FOOT'S TEAM (left to right) : Joan Lestor, wom

**VOTE
KATHLEEN SMITH**

Barwick and Kippax
Ward

**Kathleen Mary Smith
Proud Wife Happy Mother
Devoted Grandma
City Councillor since 1978
Parish Councillor since 1969**

Labour election leaflet, Leeds

EDITH CRESSON, the French farming minister, who roundly accused the British government last week of terrorist tactics in the EEC, is a trim 46-year-old with tousled red hair, high cheekbones and a devastating smile. She is much the prettiest of the politicians who jet in and out of Common Market negotiations.

Sunday Times

For a lady Mrs Thatcher has handled herself very well — for a lady.
But it is not a women's job to tackle the war situation we are threatened with.

Letter, Nottingham Evening Post

Girl talk

Margaret Thatcher and Indira Ghandi had their second and final round of formal talks in New Delhi today.

Evening Advertiser, Swindon

Commons is no place for a wife

A TORY MP, Mr Alan Clark, protested yesterday that MPs' "traditional and congenial arrangements" would be disturbed if a proposal to allow MPs' wives to have lunch in the Members' dining room went ahead.

Glasgow Herald

MR. MICHAEL FOOT, the Labour leader, will spend this morning in the canteen
He will be surrounded by many of the plant's 240-strong workforce, mostly young women: he will be impressed and they will be largely in awe.

Financial Times

SUPPORT THE CUTS!

University of Warwick Conservative Magazine

Mr Boyson: I think few people on either side of the House would advocate nursery education for all. The most any Government has done is to increase provision for those who wished it.

Many people feel that where mothers can be at home with children that is a very satisfactory situation. Nursery education has developed particularly for those children who need it.

Commons debate, The Times

I am a Conservative and I voted this Government into power. However, even before the election I felt a nagging doubt. With all due respect to my dear wife and those other few ladies who deem to speak to me, I was suspicious of a political party who could not find a man to lead them.

Letter, Stafford Newsletter

Housewife wins for Labour

Housewife Mrs. Jane Frances Mott polled 1,123 votes against the 633 votes of her Conservative opponent, Mr. Raymond Cooper, giving a comfortable majority of 490. Mrs. Mott is employed by Pirelli

Burton Daily Mail

"We have been discussing the possibility of positive discrimination for women and I don't think it is a bad idea," he said.

"On a committee of six people positive discrimination would mean there should be at least two women."

Williams Rodgers MP, Oxford Star

SDP man stands down

A candidate for the Liberal Social Democratic Alliance Mrs Ann Musselwhite is to stand down.

Mrs Musselwhite who would have stood in the Bruce Grove ward would only comment that she "no longer had any sympathy with the Alliance."

Wood Green and Tottenham Weekly Herald

WHY ALL this fuss from Ms Lesley Abdela and her 300 group about the "need" for more women MP's?

There aren't all that many women labourers, bricklayers, dustmen, and roadsweepers are there? What it all boils down to is that women only want to be equally represented in cushy, well paid jobs.

Letter, Daily Express

Lord Gisborough (C) said that the less educated a woman was, the more children she had. "Much of our riots resulted from overcrowding in poorer areas." Wives who were least able to manage their own families should be sterilised, he said.

Lords Debate, The Guardian

In my 12 years or more as Party Leader, I regularly paid tribute to our older women members all over the country for addressing envelopes, voting cards and making tea.

In constituency party meetings all over the country those ladies are now in tears, drifting away, fearing to attend, because of the bully-boys of Benn persuasion.

Harold Wilson, News of the World

TORY MP **Tim Brinton's** wife **Jeanne** is up in arms. Her application to join her local Conservative Club in Rochester has been turned down —because she is a woman.

Says Mrs Brinton, a Tory county councillor : " I was stunned. It amazes me when we have a woman Prime Minister, and our local MP is a woman, that I can't even be a proper member of the Conservative Club.

" It is a ridiculous rule and I am fighting to get it thrown out as soon as possible."

Male members of the Medway Conservative Club are less than happy with the thought of a feminine uprising. Club president, **Andy Anderson**, said : " I don't think this idea will be appreciated by many members. The women at the club do take a keen interest in things, but I'm sure they are happier with the men actually making the decisions."

Sunday Express

MR MARTYN DEARDEN, treasurer of Wessex Area Young Conservatives, speaking to Reading North Young Conservatives on the subject of "Sin in our Cities," said: "An important feature of the decline in the quality of life over the past 15 years must surely be the deterioration in generally accepted moral standards.

There is plenty of evidence in what we see reported on television and in other mass media. Plenty of publicity is given to women's-libbers and other agitators who wish to break down the fabric of society by attacking the institution of the family.

Reading Chronicle

The single-parent family was the "horror of the age," declared Yarmouth MP Sir Anthony Fell at the weekend.

He claimed the right name for a single-parent family was "someone who has given up the fight, the struggle of remaining married."

He was speaking about the decline in family responsibility at the Yarmouth and East Norfolk Conservative Association president's dinner at the Burlington Hotel, and asked: "What sort of a nation is it where mothers no longer give a damn for their kids?

"They give a damn about their second cars, first cars or colour TV sets, or whatever it may be" — and regarded them as more important than their children.

Eastern Daily Press

Ape in the Media

I TURNED for illumination to the newspapers. They hardly mentioned men at all. All over Christmas it was rape, rape, rape. Now it was interminable questionnaires in which girls under 25 stressed that careers were infinitely more important than caresses.

Jilly Cooper, Mail on Sunday

IT'S HARD to be rude to a woman, particularly if she's not ugly, says Radio Clyde Programmme Chief Alex Dickson.

Sunday Standard

WHO will watch breakfast TV when the BBC launches it early next year?

Some wives will watch it, of course, particularly if soap operas and feminine programmes are shown.
The result will be many burnt offerings in the cooker, and holes scorched in shirts as the iron is forgotten during some dramatic screen moment.

Bristol Evening Post

THIS YEAR, with your help, VSO hopes to sponsor around 500 volunteers to live, work and share their skills with Third World communities. All these volunteers have knowledge and training that are desperately needed – agriculturalists, teachers, technologists, doctors, craftsmen and women.

David Dimbleby, VSO Appeal

APART FROM improving the news supply to the lady on the other side of the marmalade pot, there's a great deal of merit in prising the back page of *The Times* away from the classifieds.

UK Press Gazette

SHOW ME the contents of a woman's shopping basket and I'll tell you what she is.

Paul Levy, The Observer

TODAY MEN associate women with pre-menstrual tension, post-menstrual depression, abortion, Lesbians Against Rape and the Equal Opportunities Commission.

Mary Kenny, Daily Mail

Who are the people mostly promoting 'women's rights' in Britain ? They are a motley group of extreme-Left liberationists, Whitehall bureaucrats (spending £2½ million every year on that silliest of Quangos, the Equal Opportunities Commission), and frustrated women, over-represented, alas, in my own profession, journalism, whose own careers or marriages have failed to be fulfilling and who seek to blame others for it.

I am absolutely convinced the vast majority of women simply do not mind a bit that the throne of our country is passed on through the male line. In fact, for a variety of reasons they would find hard to put into words, they probably like the idea.

Joanna Bogle, Daily Mail

Some people
even use them for Rubbish!

Advert for refuse sacks

really so terrible if a man makes a pass at you?
  Many a woman who's being taken for granted at home is secretly chuffed when the men at work refer, however lewdly, to her ample bosom, her sexy legs or her bedroom eyes.
  The time to worry is when chaps stop fancying you. Not when they do!

Rosalie Shann, News of the World

            young people should be out kicking a ball around, or pillaging telephone boxes, or interfering with the local maidens, or at least showing some evidence of *youth.*

Frank Johnson, The Times

            One thing I didn't know at 18 is that ladies are much randier than men. They're wandering round looking for sex the whole time but unfortunately I didn't realise that.

Reginald Bosanquet, Sunday Express

**STOP PRESS—
ALL LADIES!**
Latest cock-eyed idea at BBC TV is to have an all-female television newsreading team. The fact that this will drive away their remaining audience does not, it seems, bother them.

Girl About Town Magazine

World of Sport

JOHN LOWE has won every major title except for Bullseye. Can he make it a full cabinet for his wife to clean?

Tony Green, BBC 2 Darts Commentator

Boycott, for certain, Gooch and Gower, and hopefully Botham and Hughes are a prime five that dads might take their sons to for a day out during this Ashes season. But the most important reason for mum to make up the early morning pack of sandwiches for the family will be if Lillee is playing.

Frank Keating, The Guardian

MY PARTICULAR thanks are due to Christine Forrest who must be the only member of her sex capable of taking 200 words out of an over-long match report without upsetting its balance.

John Woodcock, Wisden Cricketers' Almanac

A FAMILY treats itself to a video so that the junior members can keep a visual record of the World Cup Final, so that dad won't miss his favourite comedies because of the darts match and so that mum can see Des O'Connor over and over again while she's doing the ironing in the morning.

Shropshire Star

IF YOU'RE not doing anything, why not invest £1 in a good night's entertainment? And, if you really feel in a good mood, why not bring the wife with you.

From Rotherham United Programme

McENROE'S EYE, you see, is nigh on perfect. Ipso facto, if he argues, he is right; the umpires and linesmen, usually old fogeys or women are wrong.

Dudley Doust, Sunday Times

WOMEN OFTEN have no ready access to a coin and experience difficulty in spinning a coin. It is therefore polite for a man to proffer a coin to a female low bisquer. She may take it and toss it, or more usually she will say: "Oh, please will you toss it. I'll call heads or tails."

Croquet customs, Croquet Gazette

FILLIES ARE like women – not to be relied upon. This is especially true early in the season.

Daily Mirror Companion to Racing

THEY WERE on strange ponies, said Graham. It is rather like going out with a new woman. You always take it easy the first time.

The Standard

ARA Newspaper

"Women are the mainstay of club cricket, providing the teas, a first-rate laundry service, and a comforting shoulder when 'hubby' makes a duck, drops a dolly catch or gets hit for six. She has her uses."

Birmingham Evening Mail

by Leonard Barden

LONDON'S girl chess prodigy, Sabrena Needham, nine, of Queen's Park Junior School, triumphed over the brainiest boys last night for the third year running.

"We never expected a result like Sabrena's. It looks as if we shan't be able to give her the top trophy as it is designated for boys."

The Standard

Sport for all — except women?

WOMEN readers may be interested to note a small paragraph in a North West Sports Council letter to Fylde Council.

Talking about "target groups" for future sport developments, it says, "The following are proposed as the basis for a rolling programme:

"The unemployed, disabled, ethnic groups, elderly.

"It is suggested that 'women' should be phased in at a later date."

Lytham St Anne's Express

PERFECTION ON EIGHT WHEELS

BEADLE have been making top quality Roller Skates for over 50 years, and is almost the oldest such manufacturer in the country!

We cater for the beginner to the confident winner of top competitions, and can "tailor-make" skates to suit individual requirements.

Our skates — all with toe-stops — are produced by craftsmen and assembled by hand.

Sponsors of
FINSBURY PARK
CYCLING CLUB

● BEADLE ROLLER SKATES

Advertisment, Sport Magazine of the Sports Council

I did notice one attempt at a joke on the noticeboard. " A Woman's Right to Cues." It turned out to be an ad for a lesbian snooker club, or at least a room above a pub where the six tables on a certain night every week are reserved solely for women.

Hunter Davies, Sunday Times

It is worrying enough when sport and showbiz become entangled ; further signs of decadence were discernible at the snooker, not just because the customary flower arrangements were missing, but also because for the first time they had drafted a lady commentator, who insulted all our intelligences by describing what the gladiators were wearing : " I think they both look particularly elegant tonight."

Benny Green, The Guardian

MAN WATCH

Steve Davis

IT'S NOT woman's bodies that are the problem, it's their minds. They just don't seem able to concentrate as well as men. Which is why they'll never break into the male preserve of championship snooker. Admittedly their shape doesn't help—big breasts can make the game very awkward—but it is that lack of mental control which finally prevents them becoming top class. Chess is another example—all the best players are men.

Sunday Standard

Unlike some male stars, all-rounder Sarah has a note of consideration. She feels sorry for the men she bowls against.

'If I bowl a man out, it's extremely damaging to his ego. I genuinely feel sorry for him.'

Back at Lord's they are creased about the whole idea. Brian Aspital, Secretary of the National Cricket Association, says women already play an invaluable part in club cricket. 'They do the tea week in and week out.'

Mail on Sunday

29

World of Medicine

Daily Telegraph

WHAT IS the popular notion of someone who is gullible enough to be taken in by a sugar pill and react to it as though given some potently active chemical? Probably that he (or more likely she) is a weak-minded hysteric, – an unstable character over-concerned with bodily health.

Behaviour, by Gordon Claridge

The professor, who asked not to be named, comes from a hospital which delivers 2,300 babies a year, and whose antenatal clinics book women in batches of 10 every 15 minutes.

'Patients are dishonest in their accounts of how long they wait – we've proved this in a survey of our own.

'I get girls in here who say they are very important, lawyers or something like that, and have to get through quickly. I don't take any notice of them.

Pulse magazine

SULPHUR CAN be used for the treatment of dysmenorrhoea, especially for specific kinds of patients. Sulphur would be used for the kind of woman who is argumentative, selfish, untidy, round-shouldered and with an unkempt appearance.

Treatment of menstrual problems, MIMS Magazine

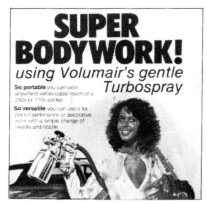

Paint spray advertisement, Journal of the Vehicle Body Repairers Associations

ECONOMY OF time may not be important for retired people or housewives, but could be very important to people leading busy working lives who feel they have "no time" to exercise.

From Look After Yourself, Health Education Council

WOMAN DOCTOR: The village medical practice has a new doctor. Not only is she a WOMAN, she joins Dr Wassell-Smith, Dr Taylor Roberts and Dr Tudor Miles.

Wimbledon Borough News

Advertisement feature, medical circular

Mummies please note.

Old medicines should be returned to the surgery or chemist for safe disposal.

Education

Black mothers who fail children

BLACK children are failing at school because their mothers are apathetic towards education, a team of researchers has decided.

Warwickshire education committee is to study the findings of the research team—from Yale university—into immigrant children in Rugby.

Education officials will discuss how to persuade mothers of ethnic minority pupils—16 per cent. of those at Rugby schools—to become more involved in education and stimulate interest and ambition among the children.

Daily Mail

THE RAMPAGES of St Saviour's were partly due to the large number of female staff, according to Chairman of the Governors, Councillor Len Tyrer. "I am not being sexist, but if you have tough kids you need tough people to deal with them. With all due respect to the ladies, they just could not cope," he said.

Liverpool Echo

WHEN I first saw women dining as guests at the high table of an Oxford College I was naturally shocked . . . wives in general do tend to clog the conversation. No one on such occasions should be allowed to bring his own wife. Someone else's wife perhaps. That would at least guarantee a second opinion.

Anthony Lejeune, Daily Mail

I AM sorry for that young man. His wife can't cook.

French O Level Translation Test, Le Bon Chemin

MOLLIE GREY

If all the girls turn Beauty Queens
An' get their dearest wishes—
Who's going to cook the food we eat
An' wash up all the dishes?

Postcard by Dennis Productions.

EXHIBIT THE logical form for the following sentences by translating them into the notation of the predicate calculus: (a) Susan is featherbrained; (b) Janet is featherbrained; (d) All women are featherbrained; (f) No man is featherbrained; (g) Some men are not featherbrained; (h) John is not featherbrained.

Page 102, Beginning Logic

APART FROM nursing and domestic service, I consider kennel work can be the best training a young girl can get for her future as a housewife.

Joe Cartledge in Dog World

TO DEVELOP self-confidence and respect, a child must know who he is, where he belongs, where his roots are. He needs a father-figure to respect and to want to emulate, and a mother-figure to love.

.., children need someone to pray with them. Too often this is left to mother, but it's important, especially for boys, for father to pray with them - they must not think that prayers are just for women

Leeds Catholic Voice

From Children of Immigrants to Britain, by Edwin Lobo

Bright boys; girls for brightening-up

Marlborough College, founded 1843. 800 boys and 85 sixth-form girls, all boarding. Roger Ellis, the Master, describes the school as "liberal and progressive". Under John Dancy, in the sixties, it was one of the first public schools to abolish fagging and to open the sixth form to girls, for whom academic ability is not the only entry requirement: "We like musicians, games players, actors: girls who will brighten the place up. Occasionally we choose a girl who's just tremendous fun"

Sunday Times Magazine

PLANS for council childminders on the rates have been dropped.

The move to open a creche at Reading Borough Council was put forward by Labour councillors. Mrs June Orton said it would help cut out "inequality" between male and female members of staff as women would be able to stay in council employment after having babies.

But Tory Fred Pugh said the idea would lead to more unemployment. He said: "If more women were at home looking after their children there would be less unemployment. It's more natural for women to be at home. Women are most fulfilled at home looking after children."

Reading Chronicle

I THINK cooking is a subject for boys and girls, for if the boys don't get married they will have to cook for themselves.

Unnamed boy on A Question of Equality BBC2

BOYS ESPECIALLY need someone who is masculine with whom thy can be rough and get dirty. Someone who is going to be less worried about torn trousers and grazed knees (after all, mother's always there to clean up) and who will encourage him to leave the safety of his mother and explore new worlds. Being there, dad can make all the difference. *Toddler's Progress*

The reduction in student numbers comes when there is a record numbers of 18-year-olds in the population and an increasing demand for university education from women and mature students.

The Guardian

The woman who's rocking the Church

ATTRACTIVE in her orange and gold brocade vestments, with just a hint of mascara and lipstick, all eyes were on E l i z a b e t h Canham yesterday as she stepped into a London pulpit to preach the sermon.

For defiantly but without fuss, Elizabeth is setting out to rock the traditions of the Church of England.

A former teacher, with degrees of B a c h e l o r of Divinity and M a s t e r of Theology, she was ordained a Priest in America

Daily Express

WE SHALL be having three competitions for all members of the congregation. We would like all to make a collage picture – the ladies using items that may be found in a sewing box, the gentlemen a picture with items from a tool box.

Link, magazine of the Trinity United Reform Church

WHILE CONCLUDING that marriage "is a parnership", Mr Rees adds that "the man is the senior partner in matters of order or functi on. It is he who is to provide for his wife and not vice versa. It is he who has to "set the tone" in the spiritual atmosphere of the home. It is he who has the ultimate responsibility for the disciplining of the children.

Vicar of St Luke's, London NW3, Hampstead and Highgate Express

Let us note that the largest part of the word progress is in fact ogress—quite sobering when we think of the ordination of women !—
Yours,
Joseph T. Cartwright.

Letter, The Guardian

SO LET us not forget. God commanded a man to rule properly over his wife (Gen. 3:16). Women increasingly these days are ruling over weak and ineffectual men contrary to God's law. God will punish both men and women for forsaking their proper roles.

Plain Truth

THE Archbishop of Canterbury's boisterous wife, **Ros Runcie, has** everything a woman could possibly need: an attentive husband, a happy family and nice little homes at St Albans and Lambeth Palace.

Daily Mirror

DR RUNCIE does not favour the ordination of women, and how right he is: women priests mean the end of Christianity as we have known it. The lady he met who had been ordained in the American Church had frizzed permed hair and pink lipstick, which hardly seemed to me to be priestly.

Mary Kenny, Daily Mail.

LIONS CLUBS are an international male organisation. Although the clubs are for men, wives and girl-friends will always have a big part to play in, for example, preparing food for senior citizens' parties or driving people to hospital.

Turners Hill Parish News

I BELIEVE women can and should be ordained. They are capable of many things. However, I have reservations about women being Bishops or in charge of a parish. I have to say I believe they should be ordained, yes, but in charge, no.

Michael Baughen, Chester Bishop Designate, Chester Chronicle.

PART-TIME guides custodians required immediately by Christ Church Cathedral. These vacancies will be of interest to the wives of graduate students.

Oxford University Gazette

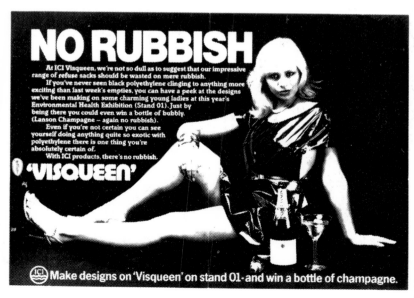

Refuse sacks advert, ICI

Arts

SIR HUGH CASSON, President of The Royal Academy, likened the academy to an abandoned spouse "visibly deteriorating and frightfully expensive to keep up".

Daily Telegraph

LAST BUT not least I would like to thank my wife who has supported me in my endeavours, has accompanied me on all journeys with the particular responsibility for travel arrangements and has undertaken the laborious task of indexing. Authors without wives cannot know what they have missed.

Acknowledgment, Flowers of Greece by Oleg Polunin

My own contender for the lemon is Tenko, the grotesquely-scripte saga of a group of women prisoners of the Japanese, which most of us watched for the first week or two to see if they showed the rape scenes in full colour.

Max Hastings, Daily Express

GIVEN PERON'S macho image there was also a contradictory feminine streak in his make-up. This took the form of childishness, a girl's girlish petulance when things went wrong, and a distinct overweening vanity.

From Evita by W. A. Harbinson

Her art makes her suffer and she doesn't realise until the film is nearly over (though we could have told her when it started) that when a woman gets what they call writer's block the block is probably sexual. That is to say, she lacks a lover.

Eric Shorter, Daily Telegraph

IN HIS first view of Presley he describes his bedroom in Graceland toward the end "propped up like a big fat woman recovering from some operation on her reproductive organs".

Elvis by Albert Goldman

"Although I'm an actress, I long ago realised that my career would have to take second place to Leonard's. It would be difficult for him if I were the star.

Gilian Raine, wife of Leonard Rossiter, Kingston and Surrey Guardian

Relationships are important for women. You can't imagine a woman being happy on her own like a man. I just think of marriage and children for girls. There's something sublimated about career women.

Stephen Spender, The Observer

I believe the only reason to get married is to have children. There is really no point in it otherwise, especially for a man. Maybe for a woman there is, because we must recognise that they do get old more quickly than men.

A 40-year-old man is a young man, but a 40-year-old lady is beginning to wonder what's going to happen to her. So she wants to get married so that she will be secure in the future. That's the reason women want to be married by the time they're about 35 — it's an attitude I meet all the time.

Sacha Distel, Sunday Standard

Hi! I'm Sandy

See me on stand 78-79.

I have several interesting things to show you!

FROM POETS like Goethe and Pushkin, or great men of action like Bismarck, down to the most brainless schoolgirl, his works were read with an almost hysterical enthusiasm.

Kenneth Clark on Byron, Civilisation

I MEAN, have you ever noticed? The only ones who ever call themselves feminists are the ugly ones. If someone is good looking they wouldn't be feminist, would they? They'd dress in nice skirts.

Harry Kakouilli, bass player with True Life Confessions, Melody Maker

If you want to level with Linda~you'll need these

BPL standard packing shims – the positive way to reduce installation time

Using components that are made for the job saves time and *that* means money.

All your fixing requirements can now be satisfied, with our complete range of shims. Designed for maximum flexibility of use, we produce singles and unique multiple composites!

Constructed from tough resilient plastic and shaped to fit around the individual fixing points the BPL shim is a must for conscientious installers.

Business News: Secretaries

It's hard to refuse a pretty girl asking to borrow a camera for the weekend. It's even harder to explain the intricacies of 35mm single lens reflex camera operation in 10 minutes. Sometimes, even focusing seems too difficult for 'phone number typewriter minds.

What Camera

The word processing boom which started in London a little over a year ago spread quickly to the North East, thanks, in no small measure, to Hazel Moodie.

Hazel, 35, petite, pretty and far too feminine for anyone to imagine that she knows about machines, has a solid computing background.

Newcastle Evening Chronicle

THE TRUE role of women in society is to exhort and inspire men to act and make suggestions with quiet confidence in order to give him courage and wisdom to meet the trials of life.

Sentence Drill, High Powered Typewriting Drills

Advert Snopake Correction Fluid

So many in the pool of potential secretaries are malcontent arts majors who can't find jobs doing anything else. They'd make wonderful mistresses but not good secretaries.

Bankers and their secretaries, from Institutional Investor

THESE ARE wines that will go down well at office parties without making the switchboard girls too giggly.

Wine ad, Law Society Gazette

AT THE lowest level we have the junior office girl who opens the incoming letters each morning. She has minimum responsibilities and we may call her decisions "vegetative."

Management and Business Studies by C. Lewis and R. Stainton

Dealing with unwanted amorous advances is more a problem for the younger girls than for senior staff. And although American secretaries are encouraged to hit back at Don Juans or even claim for sexual harassment, there are ways of getting the message across without

resorting to such drastic measures.
Don't wear plunging necklines, split-skirts or mini minis.
Don't unwittingly lead him on.
Don't be overly chatty or make jokes with dubious innuendos.
Don't accept too many after-work drinks invitations.
Don't play the wide-eyed innocent —your apparent helplessness may appeal to his manly instincts.

Advice to secretaries, Woman's Own

Advertisement, Commercial Motor

Advertisement, The Standard

Jobs

HEADMASTER AND WIFE

Beech Hall School, Macclesfield, Cheshire, is a charitable trust with a board of governors. With accommodation for at least 100 day pupils and 70 boarding pupils, it prepares boys and girls for admission at 11+ and 13+ to independent schools.

The governors wish to appoint a headmaster whose wife will accept responsibility for the school's domestic administration and the general welfare of pupils.

Times Educational Supplement

FEMINISTS have suffered a double blow with the latest micro chip wonder — a drinks machine with a male voice.

Said Jean Harvey, a spokeswoman for Klix Ltd., the manufacturers: "The voice is really a novelty and is aimed at attracting customers. We conducted tests

"Men were found to have more sensuous voices and which also have an air of authority. And women are more associated with canteens and tea trolleys."

Brighton Argus

The thought of working all day with my wife makes me shiver! Every time I went for a drink or pinched one of our office girls in fun she would be watching and noting.

No, I value my freedom too much.

News of the World

SKEGNESS COUNCIL entertainments director Leslie Shepherd is known for his progressive ideas. He was the only such official in the country to welcome a Miss Topless contest to the town.

The Stage

Councils are being urged to ensure that more local government jobs go to women and coloured people.

. . . .

But Councillor Fred Grattidge, chairman of Birmingham Personnel Committe, said: "It would be wrong to push women into positions if they are not best qualified.

"The same applies to ethnic minorities.

"They are not discriminated against. The best man gets the job."

Birmingham Evening Mail

40

The chairman of the Finance Review Sub-Committee Cllr Peter Henry said: "We have a duty to the ratepayer. It's the good old problem of employing the female of the species. It exemplifies a bit how males feel about this — the investment of training and the likelihood of a return on the investment."

NALGO News

THE SUPERIORITY in occupational achievement of men over women, even in such female areas as cooking is overwhelming . . . It seems reasonable to suppose that sex differences are brought about principally by sex chromosomes. But conclusive evidence is lacking.

A-Z of Management, Penguin Books

Redditch Advertiser

IF YOU have a leaning towards cookery, beauty, house decoration or housewifery, your specialised field is ready to hand.

Opportunities for Women, Prospectus of London School of Journalism

NALGO, the town hall union, has a film telling members what to do if cornered, propositioned, squeezed, kissed, pinched, smacked, bitten, or merely embarrassed by dirty jokes at work. Heavens knows where all this will lead. I myself am against sexual equality.

David Hamlett, Bath and West Evening Chronicle

"What is wrong with the leader of a union wanting a nice house for each of his members to live in? he asks. What is wrong with wanting a good standard of living for his wife and family, a good education for the children, a Jaguar at the front door to take him to work, and a Mini at the side to take his wife shopping?"

Joe Gormley, Battered Cherub

41

WE AIM to provide informal counselling and social education and to develop a non-sexist approach to working with young people. Applicants must be female.

Advert for Craft Workshop Organiser, The Guardian

A SPOKESMAN for United Biscuits said the company had been flooded with applications for part-time packing and process operator jobs. "Many of the applicants were men and we have pointed out to them that they would find themselves working with women. This deterred some, but others were still interested."

Hartlepool Mail

The strain that former breadwinners suffer on the dole was described yesterday by Robin SeQueira, Wirral's social services director.

They are in debt, have lost confidence in themselves and even feel subservient to wives in part-time jobs, he said.

Roger Todd, Daily Mirror

A WORKER needs more than a vague sense of contentment. He needs to feel that he is participating responsibly . . . the one exception here may be women workers who, their minds usually full of subjects out and beyond their chore, are conceivably happier doing repetitive work; even this, however, is, arguable.

The Business of Management by Robert Falk, published by the British Institute of Management

One of the main attractions for a woman is the fact she can see all the bargains in the town centre shops on her patrol as soon as they go in the windows.

Traffic wardens feature, Huddersfield Examiner

THE PART to be played by wives and girlfriends of members of a self-build group is a difficult subject to be specific upon. Very valuable work has been provided in the past in secretarial, accounting and welfare duties as well as decorating, cleaning and landscaping.

Manual for self-build housing Associations

42

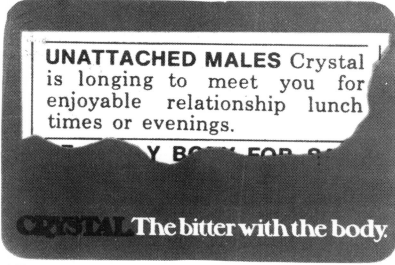

LIBBERS HAVE infiltrated the unions. The latest piece of nonsense comes from the engineering workers' union which is accusing the Offshore Operators Association of sex discrimination by operating an unofficial ban on employing women on North Sea drilling rigs. I hope such a ban exists. Women in boats have always been considered bad luck.

"Diver" in British Sub Aqua Club Magazine

FOUR women are among the latest volunteers in Brighton for a wartime bomb disposal squad.

Their applications were turned down.

"Women could do the job," said staff administration officer Capt. Brian Batty.

"But would they really want to ruin their hands and fingernails?"

Brighton and Hove Gazette

IF ALL women left work and went back to the kitchen sink there would be many more jobs available, the Mayor of Winchester, Mr Ian Bigood, told first year students at King Alfred's College. "But," he hastened to add, "I would not suggest it."

Hampshire Chronicle

THERE ARE also small business owners, voluntary workers running a variety of concerns, and housewives managing the affairs of the home. In this context it is fully recognised that women have a rightful place in management.

Foreword to Management Made Simple

AS THE machine takes over and work becomes a shrinking activity it may have to be shared out. And the first priority must be to youngsters leaving school, then to men, with ladies and "oldies" at the back of the queue. Ladies have the home and children, "oldies" have their memories.

Doug Barker, Bedfordshire Times

Business News: Finance

DECEIVE your wife next Friday—give her a dummy. pay slip.

An enterprising North Eastern printer will now sell you a forged pay slip, complete in every detail but showing your pay a good deal less than it is. Just hand this slip to your wife together with some of the contents of your pay packet. Then go out n safety and drink the

Daily Mail

The death of a breadwinner can have a tremendous financial impact on a family. No less serious is the loss of a wife, bearing in mind the escalating cost of employing a housekeeper.

Leaflet, Matthews Comfort and Co. Insurance Brokers

IS the burden of income tax crippling you? Then send your wife out to work — part time will do. Because of the tax laws, the money she earns will be worth much more than if you did the extra work yourself.

Hugh Emerson, Daily Mail

DESPITE HIS plans for retirement he might decide to use his savings – now at £4,676 – for his daughter's wedding.

Or after 15 years he might decide to use his savings – which could have multiplied to £9,059 – to send his son to a public school.

Advertisement, Lloyds Life Insurance, The Observer.

AGGRESSIVE BUSINESSMEN can easily persuade unsophisticated people, particularly housewives, to purchase goods they do not really require and cannot afford.

Commerce Made Simple

PERSONALLY I believe Legal and General's new policy might prove to be too much of a temptation to a lot of people. Well, what would you opt for, your missus or an extra ten grand a year? (By the way, paraquat is a bit suspect this year, lads. Try encouraging a suicide and blaming it on PMT).

Ackroyd column, The Advertiser, Bournemouth

BANKRUPTCY LIKE heart attack tends to strike suddenly. Inevitably, though, some people see it coming and take evasive action – trying to keep funds in the family by transferring to their wives, for instance.

Tom Tickell, Financial Guardian

Transport

Trade yours in _now_ they get expensive at this age!

IT IS interesting to note that rape in the western world is on the decline, perhaps thanks to the car as an outlet for uncontrollable behaviour for man. But as manic driving leads to more deaths, perhaps rape is to be preferred.

How to Drive, by Hugh Franks

Switch on

"There is now a fantastic range of bikes for ladies. They are automatic and easy to ride.

"I am not saying that women are thick, but like vacuum cleaners and washing machines they just like to be able to switch things on automatically."

Leicester Mercury

Whereas the bullet-like 928 could be likened to a sophisticated, slender, beautiful career girl in her twenties, full of untapped but obvious potential, the 911 turbo equates to the highly volatile attractive lady who's just a bit past it. Experienced, slightly nervous, somewhat tarted up and not beyond slapping you in the face if you go a little bit too far. Both propositions, like the 928 and the 911 turbo, offer the prospect of great pleasure.

Motoring News

THIS WILL suit the rising young executive who likes to cut a dash when he is stepping out in town during the week but who, at the weekend, is faced with the predicament of two young children and a wife.

Car Feature, THE magazine

THIS VERY modern book is ideal for young learners and women; it is packed with drawings.

Lawrence Nathan's Car Driving in Two Weeks

Advertisement, Wellingborough and Rushden Post

BEWARE! CAREFUL WOMEN DRIVERS

Sheffield Star

MEN don't expect women to drive with care and consideration, and when they do, says Stella Bruce, bang goes everyone's no-claims bonus!

DRIVERS: BELT the wife and kids – and keep them safe.   *Road Safety Poster, London E15*

47

Inner Ape

*If you are lifting spuds today
the sacks you need are*
ABERTAY

*Buy your Sacks from the only
manufacturer in East Anglia*
**Telephone WISBECH 5901
or HULL 23434**

**ABERTAY PAPER SACKS
SANDYLAND, WISBECH**

Eastern Daily Press

VIRGO (Aug 24-
Sept 22)
Virgo housewives will try
something new in the kit-
chen, while Virgo men
could be thinking of
changing their jobs.

News of the World

THE BOOK is divided into
seven sections – Scientists
and Inventors; Writers and
Poets; Leaders and
Reformers; Artists and
Musicians; Discoverers and
Explorers; Soldiers and
Statesmen; Great Women.

*Cover quote from 100 Great
Lives, by Odhams Books*

DRIVER SALVATORE
SPIRO said: She is such a good
worker we sometimes forget
she is a woman."

*Wolverhampton Express and
Star*

Mix business with pleasure.
If you want to work, we can
arrange a day at the office with
international telephone and telex
facilities.
Meanwhile, your wife can go
shopping, visit the hairdresser, watch
a movie or have a massage.

QE2 ad, Sunday Times

IT IS believed that the ladies
require three essentials for
an enjoyable holiday on a
boat – lots of sun, access to
a bath, and several visits to
the hairdresser.

*Guide to the Brecon and
Abergaveney Canal*

AMONG THE finishers (of a
five-mile sponsored run)
were a 10-year-old boy,
someone with an arthritic
hip and several girls.

Burnley Express and News

LIVELY BIOGRAPHY of
three formidable lassies:
Catherine de Medici, Diane
de Poitiers and Marguerite,
Queen of Navarre. If all
women had been as bright
as these three, we would
never have needed Mrs
Pankhurst.

*Book advertisement, The
Observer*

Norwich Union magazine

THE BBC offered to provide Colin
Watts with the music centre, plus
a black-and-white portable, and
a nice set of saucepans for Mrs
Watts to make up the value.

Dudley Castle's 1,000 - years history could be brought to life through an archaeological dig.

The scheme has received a cool response from Miss Josephine Wade, secretary of Dudley Archaeological and Historical Society.

"If people go grubbing around under the castle walls they could further ruin its foundations and I wouldn't expect there to be much in the ground anyway," she warned.

"I shouldn't think our society would help carry out the dig because we are mostly ladies," she added.

Dudley Herald

Point of order
When dining out, I always thought it correct to tell my escort what food I had chosen from the menu, and he would then tell the waiter. On television, I have noticed that ladies often order direct from the waiter. Which is correct, please?
Helen Douglas, Dorset.

Officially, your escort should order, but etiquette is based on good manners, not hard and fast formal rules. I usually turn to the waiter for his advice on a dish I fancy, say it sounds lovely, nod to my companion and leave him to order.

Letter in TV Times

YOU MAY have noticed we had two women in our team this week. Next week we will be back to normal.
David Jacobs, Any Questions

Cover, Greater Manchester guide to pensions

A LORRY formed a platform with a musician with a melodeon and a girl with a tin whistle.
The Guardian

Lady Barton, widow of Sir William Pell Barton, KCIE, CSI, died on March 21 in her 92nd year. She was Evelyn Agnes (Eve), daughter of J. C. T. Heriz Smith, and she was married on 1918. Her husband died in 1956.

The Times

FRETWELL'S ACCOMPLISHMENTS include an immense knowledge of Common Market practice, a friendly personality and a delightful wife.

Daily Telegraph

RAPE!

IS COMMITTED EVERY WEEKEND AT BRISTOL WHOLESALE FRUIT CENTRE MARKET PRICES ARE VIOLATED AND LAID BARE COME AND JOIN IN THIS MASS PLUNDER!

BETWEEN THE HOURS OF 10am – 3pm.

Ad for Bristol Wholesale Fruit Market

Woman and black to fly in shuttle

From George Alexander in Los Angeles

A woman and a black have been chosen by the National

The Guardian

Treat your wife as though she were your best client.

Hotel ad, Stockport Area Messenger

IT IS suggested that every woman correspondent to the news conference should be invited to do her family wash in one of our laundries . . . Press and television would find this idea attractive.

Edinburgh District Council minute on laundry promotion

There would be sessions for men on Tuesdays and Saturdays and for women on Mondays and Thursdays. He had chosen Saturday exclusively for men because he said women would be doing their shopping and household chores on Saturday.

New Sauna, Darlington Times

Gift idea for your wife

STUCK for a Christmas gift for your wife? Why not get her an official street map – she'll find her way to the shops much easier.

The map also has useful telephone numbers, local mileage charts, train routes,

Stockport Civic Review

I am not sure if last week's correspondent, J. Butterfield, is male or female, though the letter has a lack of logic which suggests, of course, a woman writer.

Kenneth Robinson, What's On in London

WOMEN whose husbands won't normally let them go out at nights are happy to do so if the destination is a slimming club.

Northwich Guardian

I MUST apologise to you, Miss Meacham, for elevating you earlier to "Mrs Meacham." *Magnus Magnusson, Mastermind*

AS THIS is probably the last week before Christmas when there is not much for husbands to do, except watch their wives amusing themselves by baking, cooking, sewing, ironing and dusting, there are plenty of alternatives to taking the dog to the pub.

Manchester Evening News

Repairs ad, Worcester Evening News

Want the key to our strip club?

Ryan makes turf-cutters both large and small. Rugged heavy-duty machines that will cut up to 187 feet of turf per minute, cut it into strips and roll it automatically.
And lighter machines too, suitable for more modest tasks.

Dependability is the keynote with Ryan equipment. And a reputation for getting the job done under all conditions.

So if you'd like to join our strip club and get the key to turf replacement the easy way, just clip the coupon. Ryan will have your ground topless in no time!

Please send me complete details.

Name

Address

Pk & Spts

MC Marshall Concessionaire Ltd

Oxford Road, Brackley, Northamptonshire NN13 5E
Tel: Brackley (0280) 703134 Telex 837593

Turf Cutter ad, Parks and Sports ground

53

Ape at Large

Stelrad Central Heating advert

SENORA GALTIERIE'S first reaction to the Falklands crisis was truly feminine. She dashed down to the hairdresser's.

Daily Mail

MOST GIN in this country is drunk with tonic, ice and lemon. I find this a rather unworthy, mawkish drink and best left to women, youngsters and whisky distillers.

Kingsley Amis, Daily Express

KAMLA the Indian girl bought by a Delhi journalist to expose the "flesh trade" may only have cost half the price of a buffalo. But at £130 she still seems to me rather expensive.

Alexander Chancellor, Spectator

Asbestos stripping advert

A handy bolt hole

HERE'S the answer for every nagged and hen-pecked husband — escape to your nearest evening centre this autumn. Better still, if she mithers again about that broken shelf or loose gasket pack her off to one of the DIY or car maintenance classes.

Either way evening classes are well worth the money. Not only could they save you a fortune, they could also save you peace of mind, let alone your marriage!

Civic Review, Stockport

The textures are similar, the colours are varied, and they all have different degrees of resistance.

Wareite Xcel Boards

AFTER A woman, a pipe is a man's most treasured possession.

Eskdale   and   Liddesdale Advertiser

THE PLACE is like a fashion show as countless young lovelies (and the odd bit of mutton) swirl past the open air tavernas . . .

Summer Holiday Brochure

Good: Valid, Sound, Thorough, Ample, Considerable (gave her a *good* beating). . .

Concise Oxford Dictionary

RUSSIAN Valentina Tereshkova became the first woman in space 19 years ago today in Vostok 6, when she was 26.

News of the World

Julia Becker has created a little piece of history by being elected the first female chairman of the Brent Cross Teenage Centre, which meets at Golders Green Synagogue.

However, wounded male egos may be assuaged by the knowledge that Julia is in a minority on the new committee.

Jewish Chronicle

In contrast to the popular feminist myth of an Indian wife as no more than a chattel, Mrs Bhargarva seemed her husband's partner in every sense. While her husband answered the phone and consulted two thick files marked "Hindu Girls" and "Sikh Girls," Mrs Bhargarva fluttered round me with cups of tea. She took her duty to the clients very seriously.

The Standard

HUNDREDS of angry women demonstrated for two hours outside a dry cleaner's.

The offending owner had put up a sign which said: "Men! Why bother to get married? We'll wash your shirts, press your pants and sew your buttons on."

One of the protestors in Baltimore, Maryland, said: "The owner should consider unmarried women who want a husband. He's ruining our chances with his stupid sign."

Weekend

Practical Photography

Tokina up front

THE FIRST baby boy has been born in the village of Wittenham, Oxfordshire, for 18 years. Some villagers had blamed the "girls only" jinx on the water supply and a nearby Atomic Energy Research Establishment.

Daily Mail

If your old china is all she's cracked up to be, you'd like her replaced as new.

Sun Alliance ad, The Guardian

Ambivalence: a mixture of love and hatred for the same person at the same time; usually used in reference to mother-in-law.

Webster's New School and Office Dictionary

ARMY APPLICATION form part B/2: Names and addresses of two responsible persons (three in the case of women's services) . . .

Forces recruitment form

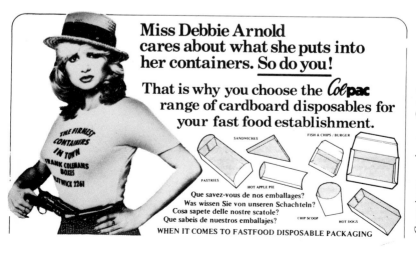

Miss Debbie Arnold cares about what she puts into her containers. So do you!

That is why you choose the *Col***pac** range of cardboard disposables for your fast food establishment.

SANDWICHES

FISH & CHIPS / BURGER

PASTRIES

HOT APPLE PIE

Que savez-vous de nos emballages?
Was wissen Sie von unseren Schachteln?
Cosa sapete delle nostre scatole?
Que sabeis de nuestros emballajes?

CHIP SCOOP

HOT DOGS

WHEN IT COMES TO FASTFOOD DISPOSABLE PACKAGING

Containers advert, Catering magazine

Chain her up for £8

It's Gold sale time at David John.
and our prices are
tumbling on a magnificent range
of chains, earrings, pendants,
bracelets and rings.
We buy in such large quantities to
stock our 8 shops that when we have a
sale, you get a gift!
Come on into David John, now and
see our Golden Sale.

MOST OFFICE parties seem to be events of quite stupefying gentility. conversation seems to be sporadic and, such is the tedium to which life has been reduced by militant feminism, totally banal.

Lord Chalfont, Executive World

MANY CORRESPONDENTS are unduly concerned with nuclear warfare. Rather they should concern themselves more with the abysmal moral standard of today's "liberated" women and the subsequent damage done to the family life and national harmony.

Letter, Bristol Evening Post

MARRIED WOMEN travelling unaccompanied must produce a duly certified or legalised letter of approval from their husband.

Visa application form, Zaire

58

Pork Scratchings packet

APPLICATIONS ARE now invited for this year's annual dinner. The dinner's essential character will be maintained — it will be for men only.

Letter to members, London Maritime Arbitrators Association

It may inherit the scientific mind of its father. the musical ear of a grandparent or the athletic prowess of some other member of the family. Or just the beautiful blue eyes of its mother.

Diana Hutchinson, Daily Mail

Britain is like an old mistress and should be treated with love and respect, even if she has faded a bit.

Carlos Fuentes, The Guardian

Boiler maintenance advertisement, *Western Gazette*

THE FIRST thing to understand about women's liberation is that it is basically a conspiracy of ugly women against pretty women.

Gerald Warner, Sunday Standard

Hysteria: Disturbance of a woman's nervous system with convulsions. . .

Collins English Gem Dictionary

AUSTRALIAN OUTLOOK   Page 19

Thin and dim women in favour with Australian men

WOMEN who are intelligent or fat — or, worse still, both — are out of favour with Australian men when it comes to choosing a companion.

But the fun-loving woman still scores high in the marriage stakes and has an excellent chance of making it to the winning post — provided she is not too bright and keeps her figure in good order.

lished this week, showed that men there were more wary of an "intelligent" professional partner than 10 years ago.
...g about West Coun-

the women's physical aspect, especially they do not want anyone who is overweight. And personality: they want someone who is outgoing and fun-

files than intelligent men".

She reports, as did the British bureau, that more me are inclined to take sing' mothers.

Australian Outlook

60

FOUR of the last five chairmen of Brighton and Hove Debating Society have been women — despite the fact that the majority of members are men.

Bill Mason, the society's secretary, has put forward a possible explanation.

"We all know that women talk more than men."

Brighton and Hove Leader

Intuition: Untutored intelligence, illogic, feminine reason, feminine logic . . .

Roget's Thesaurus

"Everyone likes to think there are snooker groupies around. There are girls there for the taking, but it's not much of a conquest going off with them. So I don't bother.

"It's a symbolic game. It's a cruel game. And let's face it, the majority of women like to be dominated.

TEN LIVELY lasses have been chosen to represent the company. They've had special training in how to look pretty while opening a can of Britvic orange juice.

Britvic news release

Pumps service advertisement

BIG JUNE THEY CALL ME – AND YOU SHOULD SEE WHAT I'VE GOT FOR ALL PARKRAY INSTALLERS!

Big June will really get you going this summer. Buy your new season's Parkrays early and you'll be amazed at the great gifts that Big June will bring… Send off the coupon – find out more – Big June will give you all the hot news!

Ⓣ Parkray

…trust it

TI Parkray Limited, Park Foundry, Belper, Derby DE5 1WE
(0773-82) 3741

I'd like to know a bit more about Big June.
Let me have the bare facts.

Name ....

Company Name ....

Domestic Heating and Plumbing